CW00615986

for Dennis with best wishes &
thanks

John

23x '07

John Seed

Also by John Seed:

Spaces In (Pig Press, Newcastle-upon-Tyne 1977)
History Labour Night. Fire & Sleet & Candlelight (Pig Press, Durham 1984)
Transit Depots (Ship of Fools, London 1993)
Interior in the Open Air (Reality Street, London 1993)
Divided into One (Poetical Histories, Cambridge 2003)
New & Collected Poems (Shearsman, Exeter 2005)
Pictures from Mayhew: London 1850 (Shearsman, Exeter 2005)

—John Seed—

That Barrikin

Pictures from Mayhew II

First published in in the United Kingdom in 2005 by
Shearsman Books Ltd
58 Velwell Road
Exeter EX4 4LD

www.shearsman.com

ISBN-13 978-1-905700-52-3

ISBN-10 1-905700-52-0

Cover and title page based on designs by poppodomedia.com

Acknowledgements
Some parts of this book have previously appeared, sometimes in
earlier versions, in *The Argotist Online* (www.argotistonline.co.uk); *Fire*;
Intercapillary Space (http://intercapillaryspace.blogspot.com); *The Poetry
Buzz, London, 23rd July 2005*; *Signals* (www.signalsmagazine.co.uk); *Staple
Magazine*. The interview that closes the book is reproduced by permission
of Edmund Hardy.

COAL HEAVERS

AUTHOR'S NOTE: Every word in the pages that follow is drawn from Henry Mayhew's writings on London published in the *Morning Chronicle* from 1849 to 1850, then in 63 editions of his own weekly paper, *London Labour and the London Poor* between December 1850 and February 1852 and then in the four volume work of the same title. The visual images are taken from the latter.

JS

The Street-Seller of Crockery Ware

Bartering for Old Clothes

Hot spiced gingerbread! hot
spiced gingerbread!

buy my
spiced gingerbread!

sm-o-o-o-o-king hot!

hot spiced gingerbread

If one'll warm you
wha-at'll a
pound do?

Wha-a-a-at'll a
pound do?

I

1

Ah! you should come here of a summer's morning
& then you'd see 'em
sitting tying up
young & old
upwards of a hundred
poor things

thick as crows in a ploughed field

It couldn't be much
if they all of them decamped
though it aint their fault poor things

when they keeps away from here
it's either the workhouse
or the churchyard as
stops them

2

Ah! Mrs. Dolland
can you keep yourself warm?

it bites the fingers like biling water it do

II

1

I sold three times as
many potatoes as I do
now four years back I
don't know why 'cept it
be the rot set people
again them & their tastes
gone another way I sell
a few more greens than
I did but

not many

2

Such a day as this sir
when the fog's like a cloud come down
people looks very shy at my taties very

they've been more suspicious
ever since the taty rot

I thought I should never have rekivered it never

not the rot

3

Some customers is very pleasant with me
& says I'm a blessing

one always says he'll give me a ton of taties
when his ship comes home 'cause
he can always have a hot murphy to his cold saveloy
when tin's
short

4

They don't live long
diseased as they are they

eat salt by basons-full
& drink a great quantity of water after

frequently known those who could
not have been hungry
eat cabbage-leaves
& other refuse from the ash-heap

5

It's about three years since
heard a bitter old Englishwoman say
to hell with your taty-pot
they're only meat for pigs

sure then said a young Irishman
a nice cute fellow
sure then ma'am
I should be after offering
you a taste

I heard that myself sir

6
some of these
poor fellows would
declare to God
that they hadn't
the value of
a halfpenny even
if you heard
the silver chink
in their pockets

7
I can't say they were well off sir
but they liked bread & herrings
or bread & tea
better than potatoes
without bread
at home

III

1

Then there's grass
that's often good money I
buy all mine at Covent-garden
sold in bundles
six to ten dozen squibs you
have to take home
untie
cut off the scraggy ends
trim & scrape
& make them level

in the court where I live
children help me I
give them a few ha'pence
though they're eager enough
to do it for nothing
but the fun

2

Well now sir about grass
there's not a
coster in London I'm sure
ever tasted it &
how it's eaten puzzles us

I was once at the Surrey
& there was some
macaroni eaten on the stage & I thought
grass was eaten in the same way perhaps
swallowed like one o'clock

3
I have the grass it's always called
cried in the streets

Spar-row gra-ass

tied up in bundles of a dozen
twelve to a dozen or one over

& for these I never
expect less than 6d.

for a three or four dozen lot in a
neat sieve I ask 2s. 6d.
& never take less than 1s. 3d.

I once walked thirty-five miles with grass
& have oft enough
been thirty miles

I made 7s. or 8s. a day by it

& next day

or two perhaps

nothing or maybe

one customer

IV

1

My rounds are
always in the suburbs

I sell neither in the streets nor
squares in town

I like it best where there are detached villas

& best of all where there are kept mistresses
they are the best of all customers
to men like me

we talk our customers over &
generally know who's who

one way we know the kept ladies is
they never sell cast-off clothes as
some ladies do for
new potatoes or early peas

2

Bless you sir if I
see a smart dressed servant girl
looking shyly out of the street-door
or through the area railings

& I can get a respectful word in
& say my good young lady
do buy of a poor fellow we
haven't said a word to your servants
we hasn't seen any on 'em

then she's had sir for
one penny at least &
twice out of thrice
that good young lady
chloroforms her

3

Cowcumbers were an aristocratic sale
four or five years ago they were
looked upon
first in with a beautiful bloom on them
the finest possible relish but
the cholera came in 1849
& everybody
specially the women
thought it was in cowcumbers

I've known cases
foreign & English
sent from the Borough Market for manure

4

I've mostly kept a stall
myself but I've known gals
as walk about with apples
as told me the weight
of the baskets is sich
the neck cricks & when
the loads took off its
just as if you'd a
stiff neck & the head
feels light as a feather

V

I've known young couples buy fowls to
have breakfast eggs from them one young
lady told me to bring her six
couples I knew would lay I told
her she'd better have five hens to
a cock & she didn't seem pleased
I'm sure I don't know why I
hope I'm always civil I told her
there would be murder if there was
a cock to every hen I supplied
her & made 6s. by the job

VI

Vy sir can you
tell me ow many
peoples in London

I don't know
nothing vatever
about millions but

there's a cat to
every ten people aye &
more than that so

sir you can
reckon there's not near
half so many

dogs as cats
I must know
for they all knows

me & I sarves about
200 cats &
70 dogs

VII

1

My best customers are working people that's
fond of birds its the
ready penny with them &
no grumbling

I've lost money by trusting noblemen

of course I blame their servants

you'd be surprised sir
to hear how often rich folks houses
when they've taken their turf or
what they want they'll
take credit & say
O I've got no change or
I can't be bothered with hapence or
you must call again

they can't know how
poor men has to
fight for a bit of bread

2

The weather most dreaded
when hoar frost lies long &
heavy on the ground the turf
cut with the rime upon it
soon turns black

foggy dark weather the days clips it
uncommon short & people won't
buy by candlelight
no more will the shops

birds has gone to sleep then &
them that's fondest on them says
we can get fresher turf
tomorrow

the gatherers can't work by moonlight clover
leaves shuts up like the lid of
a box & you can't tell them

3

I don't
complain so
it's nothing to nobody
what I makes

from Beever Town to
Stamford Hill &
on to Tottenham & Edmonton
turning off Walthamstow way
is as good a round as any I
goes all ways

I dont know what sort of peoples my
best customers

two of em I've been told is
banker's clerks so
in course
they is rich

VIII

1

We doesn't
dulterate
our goods like
the tradesmen it
wouldn't be easy
to dulterate cabbages
or oysters but

we deals fair
to all thats
fair to us

& thats more
than many a
tradesman does
for all their juries

2

a governor
in our line
leaves the knowledge of
all his dodges
to his son

jist as the rich

coves do their

tin

3

Why I can cheat any man I can

manage to measure mussels so

as you'd think you got a lot over

but theres a lot under measure

for I holds them up with my fingers

& keep crying mussels

full measure live mussels

I can do the same

with peas I delight to

do it with

stingy aristocrats

4

we don't work slang in the City

people know what they're a buying on there

theres plenty of us would

pay for an inspector of weights

I would

we might do fair
without an inspector
& make as much
if we only agreed
one with another

5
How's it possible
for people to live
when there's their own son
at the end of the court
a-calling his goods
as cheap again as we
can afford to sell ourn

6
I wish I knew
how the shopkeepers manage
their fruit I should like
to be up to some of
their moves they do
manages their things so
plummy

7
I've boiled oranges
& sold them to Irish hawkers

as wasn't wide awake
for stunning big uns

the boiling swells the oranges
& makes em look finer
but it spoils them
for it takes out the juice

people can't find that out though
until it's too late

I boiled the oranges
only a few minutes
three or four dozen a time

8
Its astonishing
how few people
ever complain of

having been took in it
hurts their feelings
to lose a halfpenny

but it hurts their pride
too much when they're had
to grumble in public about it

9

I don't know how it is
but we sell ing-uns
& all sorts of fruits
& vegetables
cheaper than they can buy them
where they're grown

& green walnuts too
when you'd think they had only
to be knocked
off a tree

10

Costers are often obliged
to sell things for
what they gave for them

the people haven't got
money to lay out

they tell us so

& if they are poor
we must be poor too

IX

1

Can you wonder at it I
hate the police they
drive us about we must
move on we can't stand here
& we can't pitch there

but if we're cracked up
forced to go into the Union
why the parish gives us money
to buy a barrow or a shallow
or to hire them & leave the
house & start for ourselves

& whats the use of that
if the police
won't let us sell our goods?

2

but the worst of hair is
always getting
cut off in quod

all
along of
muzzling the bobbies

3

If any one steals anything from
me & I catch him
I take it out of him on the spot

I gives him a good hiding &
there's an end of it

I know very well sir costers are
ignorant men but in
my opinion our never going to law
shows in *that* point
we are in advance of the aristocrats

never heard of a coster in a law court
unless he was in trouble
for assaulting a crusher or
anybody he'd quarrelled with
or something of that kind

X

Sometimes when we had'nt no grub
at all the other lads would
give us some of their bread
& butter but often our stomachs
used to ache with hunger &
we'd cry when we was werry
far gone & when it was
dark we'd lie down on the
bed & try & sleep until
she came home with the food

XI

He was an out & out sort

& if he knew you & he could
judge according to the school you belonged to
if he hadn't known you long he
was friendly for a bob or two
& sometimes for a glass

he knew the men that was stickers though
& there was no glass for them

why some of his customers sir
would have stuck to him long enough
if there'd been a chance of another glass
supposing they'd managed to get *one*
& then would have asked him
for a coach home

when I called on him he
used to say in his north country way he
wasn't Scotch but somewhere north of England
& he was pleasant with it well
damn you how are you?

he got the cream of the pail sir

XII

1

I never go to church
used to go
when I was a little child

at Sevenoaks I suppose I was
born somewhere thereabouts
I've forgot

what the inside of a church is like
there's no costermongers
ever go to church

except the rogues of them
that wants
to appear good

2

I was brought up a Roman Catholic
& was christened one

never go to mass now you
gets out of the way of
such things having to fight for

a living as I have it

seems like mocking going to chapel

when you're grumbling in your soul

THE LUCIFER MATCH GIRL

[*From a Daguerreotype by* BEARD]

XIII

We weren't a bit
afraid & perhaps that
was the reason
so few costers
died of the cholera

I knew them all in Lambeth
I think
& I knew only one
die of it

& he drank hard
poor Waxy

XIV

1

It's a great bother sir
a man having to provide a shed for his roots

it wouldn't do at all
to have them in the same room as we sleep in
they'd droop

I have a beautiful big shed
& a snug stall for a donkey in a corner of it
but he won't bear tying up
he'll fight against tying all night
& if he was loose why in course
he'd eat the flowers I put in the shed

the price is nothing to him he'd
eat the Queen's camellias if he could get at them
if they cost a pound a-piece so

I've a deal of trouble
must block him up somehow

but he's a first-rate ass

2

It's all nonsense to call donkeys stupid

them's stupid that calls them so

they're sensible

not long since I worked Guildford with my donkey-cart
& Jack was slow & heavy coming back

until we got in sight of the lights
at Vauxhall-gate

& then he trotted on like
one o'clock he
did indeed

just as if he smelt it was London
& knew
he was home

3

a friend of mine
doing a little work on a Sunday morning
at Wandsworth & his donkey
fell down dead

he thought he wouldn't leave the poor creature he'd
had a good while &
been out with in all weathers
by the roadside so

he dropped all notion of doing business
& with help got the poor dead thing
into his cart its head
lolloping over the end of the
cart & its poor eyes
staring at nothing

but the church-bells struck up &
up came a crusher &
took the man up

& next day he was fined 10s

can't exactly say for what

he never saw no more of the animal
& lost his stock
as well as his donkey

XV

I've nothing to complain of about the
police oft enough if I could be
allowed ten minutes longer on a Saturday
night I could get through all my
stock without loss about a quarter to
twelve I begin to halloo away as
hard as I can & there's plenty
of customers lay out never a farthing
till that time & then they can't
be served fast enough so they get
their fish cheaper than I do if
any halloos out that way sooner we
must all do the same anything rather
than keep fish over a warm Sunday

XVI

1

Why bless your soul sir
there always
was bummarees

& there always will be

just as Jack there
is a rough

& I'm a blessed bobber

2

Theres a great call
for haporths & pennorths
of lobster or crab by children
that's their claws I
bile them all myself &
buy them alive I can
bile twenty in half an hour
over a grate in a back-yard

lobsters don't fight or
struggle much in the hot water
if they're properly packed its

very few knows how to bile a lobster
as he should be biled

I wish I knew any way of
killing lobsters before
biling them I can't
kill them without smashing them to
bits & that won't do at all

3
I kill my crabs
before I bile them I
stick them in the throat
with a knife they're
dead in an instant

some sticks them with a skewer but
they kick a good while
with the skewer in them

its a shame to
torture anything
when it can be helped

4
If I didn't kill the crabs they'd
shed every leg

in the hot water they'd
come out as bare of
claws as this plate I've
known it oft enough

though I kill them uncommon quick a
crab will be quicker &
shed every leg
throw them off in the
moment I kill them but
that doesn't happen
once in fifty times

5
whelks'll boil
after they're dead & gone you see sir
as if they was alive & hungry

they never kicks as
they boils like lobsters or crabs they
takes it quiet

a missionary cove said to me
why don't you kill them first
its murder

they doesn't suffer
I've suffered more with a toothach
than the whole of a measure of whelks has
in a boiling

that I'm clear on

XVII

1

I was in the
s'rimp trade since I
was a girl I
don't know how long
I don't know how
old I am I
never knew but I've
two children one's six
& t'other's near
eight both girls I
kept count of that
as well as I can

2

My husband sells fish
in the street so
did father but he's
dead we buried him
without help of the
parish as many gets
that's something to say

XVIII

1

As far as I know sir it's
the best Hackney way
& Stoke Newington

& Dalston & Balls Pond

& Islington

where the gents that's in banks the
steady coves of them
goes home to their teas & the missuses
has muffins to
welcome them that's
my opinion

2

People likes them warm sir
to satisfy them they're fresh
& they almost always *are* fresh but
it can't matter so much
their being warm as they
have to be toasted again

I only wish good butter

was a sight cheaper

& that would make the muffins go

butter's half the battle

3

I turns out with muffins & crumpets sir

in October &

continues until it gets well into the spring

I carries a fust-rate article

werry much so if you

was to taste em sir

you'd say the same

if I sells three dozen muffins

at ½*d*. each

& twice that in crumpets

it's a werry fair day werry fair

all beyond that is a *good* day

the profit on the three dozen & the others

is 1*s*. but thats a great help

really a wonderful help to mother

for I should be only mindin the shop at home

perhaps I clears 4s. a week
perhaps more perhaps less but
thats about it sir

some does far better than that
& some
can't hold a candle to it

if I has a hextra day's sale
mother'll give me 3d. to
go to the play & that
hencourages a young man you know sir

4
My best customers is genteel houses
'cause I sells a genteel thing I
likes wet days best
'cause there's werry respectable ladies
what don't keep a servant
& they buys to save themselves going out

we're a great conwenience
to the ladies sir a great conwenience
to them as
likes a slap-up tea

5
I don't sell
or very seldom
indeed at other
times & only
in summer &
when its fine

XIX

1

Well then
consider the plum-puddings

why at least there's
a hundred thousand of 'em
eaten in London through the Christmas
& the month following

that's nearly one pudding to every

every

twenty of the population

is it sir well

perhaps that's too much but

then there's the great numbers eaten at public dinners
& suppers
& there's more plum-pudding clubs
at the small grocers & public-houses
than there used to be so

say

full a hundred thousand
flinging in any mince-pies that
may be decorated with ever-greens

well sir

every plum-pudding will have a sprig of holly in him

if it's bought just for the occasion it
may cost 1*d.* to be
really prime & nicely berried
if it's part of a lot why
it won't cost a halfpenny

so

reckon it all at a halfpenny

what does that come to

above £200

think of that then

just for sprigging puddings

2

Then look what's spent on
a Christmasing the churches
why now
properly to Christmas St. Paul's

I say *properly* mind
would take £50 worth

at least

aye more
when I think of it

nearer £100

I hope there'll be
no No Popery nonsense
against Christmasing this year

I'm always sorry when
anything of that kind's afloat

it's frequently a
hindrance to business

3

It's hard work
is Christmasing but
when you have neither money nor work
you must do something so
the holly may come in handy

it's often slow work
for you must wait sometimes
till no one's looking
& then you must work away like anything

I'd nothing but a sharp knife I borrowed
& some bits of cord
to tie the holly up

you must look out sharp
because a man
very likely
won't like his holly-tree to be stripped

moonlight nights the thing sir

when you knows where you are

4

Last December I remember a servant-girl
& she weren't such a girl either
running after me in a regular flutter
to tell me the family had forgot
to order 2s. worth of mistletoe of me
to be brought next day

oh yes sir the servant-girls they
generally have a little giggling
about it if I've said
what are you laughing at
they'll mostly say
me
I'm not laughing

5

I never goes for mizzletoe

I hardly knows it when I sees it

the first time I was out a man
got me to go for some in a orchard
& told me how to manage
but I cut my lucky in a minute
something came over me like I
felt sickish

6

I never lost my Christmas
but a little bit of it
once

two men took it & said
I ought to thank them
for letting me off without a jolly good jacketing
as they was gardeners

I believes they was men
out a-Christmasing as I were

it was a dreadful cold time that
& I was wet & hungry
& thirsty too for all I was so wet

& I'd to wait a-watching in the wet

I've got something better to do now
& I'll never go a-Christmasing again
if I can help it

7

But it ain't no good
you must often go a good way

I never knows anything
about how many miles &
if it's very ripe
it's soon shaken

there's no sure price
you may get 4d. for a big branch
or you must take 1d.

I may have made 1s. on a round
but hardly ever more

8
it can't be got near hand

there's some
stunning fine trees at the
top of the park there
t'other side of the logical Gardens but
there's always a cove
looking after them they say
night & day

XX

1

I make farthing's-worths
of sweet-stuff
for children but

I don't like it

it's an injury to trade

I was afraid
when half-farthings
was coined they'd
come among children
& they'd want
half a farthing
of brandy-balls

2

there's a gentleman sometimes
has a minute's chat with me
as he buys a penn'orth to
take home to his children

every reasonable man ought to
marry & have children
for the sake of the sweet-trade but

it ain't the women's fault
that many's single still when
one gentleman I knows buys brandy-balls
he says quite grave what
kind o' brandy do you put in them
not a drop of British says I
I can assure you not a single drop

he's not finely dressed
indeed he's a leetle seedy but
I know he's a gentleman
or what's the same thing if he ain't rich
for a common fellow 'll
never have his boots polished that way
every day of his life

his blacking bills must come
heavy at Christmas

3
An old fellow that
hasn't a stump of a tooth in front
why *he'll* stop &
buy a ha'porth of hard-bake
& he'll say
I've a deal of the boy left about me still

he doesn't show it anyhow in his look

4

I'm sometimes a thinking
I'll introduce a softer sort of toffy
boiled treacle
such as they call Tom Trot in some parts

but it's out of fashion now

it was rolled in a ha'penny stick sir
& sold stunnin'

XXI

1

I've sat with an umbrella
these seven or eight years I suppose it is

my husband's a penny lot-seller
just a middling pitch

in the summer I do a little
in engravings when I'm not
minding my husband's lots
he has sometimes a day
& oftener a night with portering
& packing for a tradesman that's
known him long

well sir I think I sell most coloured

Master Toms wasn't bad last summer

Master Toms was pictures of cats
sir you must have seen them

& I had them different colours

if a child looks on with its
father very likely it'll want pussy

& if the child cries for it
it's almost a sure sale
& more I think indeed I'm sure
with men than with women

women knows the value of money
better than men for men
never understand what housekeeping is

I have no children thank God or
they might be pinched poor things

2
Queens & Alberts & Wales's
& the other children
isn't near so good as they was

there's so many fine portraits given away
with the first number of this or that
people's overstocked

if a working-man can buy a newspaper
or a number why of course
he may as well have a picture with it

they gave away glasses of gin
at the opening of that baker's shop there
& it's the same doctrine

3

I used to keep a sharp look-out sir
for wind or rain &
many's the time them devils o' boys

God forgive me they's on'y poor children but
they *is* devils
has come up to me & said

one in particler
standin' afore the rest
it'll thunder in five minutes old bloke so

hup with yer humbereller & go 'ome
hup with it jist as it is it'll show stunnin
& sell as yer goes

O they're a shocking torment sir
nobody can feel it like people in the streets
shocking

XXII

The working-tailor's comfortable first-floor
at the West-end is redolent with the perfume
of the small bunch of violets that stands in
a tumbler over the mantel-piece

The sweater's wretched garret is rank with
the stench of filth & herrings

In the one you occasionally find small
statues of Shakspere beneath glass shades

in the other all is dirt & foetor

1

There's one old gentleman
a little way out of town he
always gives 1s.

for the first violet root
that any such as me
carries there

I'm often there
before any others Ah!
he says

here you are
you've come like Buonaparte
with your violet

I don't know exactly
what he means I
don't like to ask him you see

though he's civil he's
not what you may call
a free sort of man

2
Violets have a good sale I've
sold six dozen roots in a day
& only half as many primroses
& double-daisies
if half

everybody likes violets

I've sold some to
poor people in town but
they like their roots in pots
they haven't a bit of a
garden for 'em

more shame too I say
when they pays
such rents

3

people sits working all day
is very fond of a sweet flower

a gentleman that's always a-writing
or a-reading in his office he's
in the timber-trade
buys something of me
every time I see him twice
or thrice a week

sometimes I can't say what he
does with them all

busy men never buy
flowers as far as I've seen

4

I don't do much
for working-men the women's
my best customers

there's a shoemaker to be sure
comes down sometimes with his old woman
to lay out 2*d.* or 3*d.* on me

let's have something that
smells strong he'll say

stronger than cobbler's wax
though I can't smell that
others can I've sold him
musks as often as anything.

5
I'd rather sell polyanthuses
at a farthing a piece profit
to poor women
if I could get no more
than I'd work among
them screws that's so
fine in grand caps
& so civil they'd
skin a flea for his hide & tallow

6
I sell flowers sir
we live almost on
flowers when they are
to be got I
sell & so does
my sister all kinds
but it's very little
use offering any that's
not sweet I think

it's the sweetness as
sells them I sell
primrose when they're in
& violets & wall-flowers
& stocks & roses
of different sorts &
pinks & carnations &
mixed flowers & lilies
of the valley &
green lavender & mignonette
but that I do
very seldom & violets
again at this time
of the year for
we get them both
in spring & winter

7

I do a goodish bit in giving flowers for old clothes

I very seldom do it but to ladies

I deal mostly with them for their husbands' old hats
or boots or shoes yes sir & their trowsers
& waist-coats sometimes
very seldom their coats
& ladies boots & shoes too

there's one pleasant old lady & her two daughters
they'll talk me over any day
got me to
take togs that
didn't bring the prime cost of my roots
& expenses

they called them by such fine names that
I was had

then they was so polite O my good man
says one of the young daughters I
must have this geranium in change
it was a most big & beautiful Fairy Queen
well worth 4s.
the tog I didn't know what they called it
a sort of cloak
fetched short of half-a-crown

8
When a poor woman
or poor man either
but its mostly the women
can buy a mignonette pot
all blooming & smelling
for 1d. why
she won't bother to buy seeds

& set them in a box or a pot
& wait for them to
come into full blow

selling
seeds in the streets
can't be done so well now sir

9
There are some people
who will buy antirrhinum
& artemisia & digitalis

& wouldn't hear of snapdragon
or wormwood or foxglove
though they're the
identical plants

                    Please gentleman
                    Do buy my flowers
                    Poor little girl! Please
                    kind lady buy my violets O
                    do! please! Poor little girl!
                    Do buy a bunch please
                    kind lady!

XXIII

the great props of poaching were
the rich the poor couldn't buy
game there was a West-end
as well as a City trade
I've bought game of a country
poultry-hawker when I lived in
the City at the beginning of
this century 5s. a brace was
no uncommon price in the City
I've given as much as 10s.
for a pheasant for a Christmas
supper the hawker before offering the
birds for sale used to peer
about him though we were alone
in my counting-house & then
pull his partridges out of his
pockets & say sir do you
want any very young chickens for
so he called them hares he
called lions & they cost often
enough 5s. each of the hawker
the trade had all the charms
& recommendations of a mystery &
a risk about it like smuggling

XXIV

1

I was a gentleman's footman when I was a young
man
& saw life in town & country
I knows what things belongs I
never liked the confinement of service
the upper servants takes on so

the others puts up with it
more than they would I suppose
because they hopes to be butlers
themselves in time the only
decent people
in the house I lived in last was
master & missus

2

I couldn't settle to nothing long I'm
of a free spirit you see I was
hard up at last I
popped my watch for a sovereign because
a friend of mine we sometimes
drank together of a night
said he could put me in the pigeon & chicken line
that was what he called it but

it meant game this
just suited me for I'd been
out with the poachers when I was a lad
& when I was in service
out of a night on the sly
so I knew they got stiffish prices

3
I sold my game pigeons there was
all sorts of names for them in
the City & sometimes in the Strand
or Charing-cross
or Covent-garden
sold to shopkeepers oft enough I've been
offered so much tea for a hare

sometimes a hare in each
pocket but they was
very awkward carriage
if one was sold the other
sagged so

4
I have a tidy bit of connection now
in game & don't touch poultry
when I can get game

grouse is the first thing I
get to sell they are
legal eating
on the 12th of August but

there's hundreds of braces
sold in London that day &
they're shot in Scotland & Yorkshire &
other places where there's moors

in course they're killed
before it's legal

5
lord sir gentlefolks
& I serve a good many
leastways their cooks &
now & then themselves
they don't make a fuss about Game Laws
they've too much sense

6
In very hard weather I've
done well on wild ducks

they come over here
when the weather's a clipper

cold weather suits some birds
& kills others it aint hard weather
that's driven them here
the frost has
drawed them here
because it's only then
they're cheap I've bought
beauties at 1s. a piece &
one day I cleared 10s. 6d. out of
twelve brace of them I've often
cleared 6s. & 7s. at least
as often as there's been a chance

I knew a man
did uncommon well on them he
once told a parson or a
journeyman parson I don't know
what he was if
ever *he* prayed it was for
a hard winter & lots of wild ducks

7
Eat my own game?
if it's high?

No sir never I couldn't
stand such cag-mag my

stomach couldn't

though I've been a gentleman's servant

such stuff

don't suit nobody but rich people

whose stomach's diseased

by over-feeding

that's been brought up to it like

THE LONDON COFFEE-STALL

[*From a Daguerreotype by* BEARD]

XXV

I've been mostly on rabbits
they're Hampshire rabbits but I
don't know where Hampshire is
I know they're from Hampshire
they're called Wild Hampshire
rabbits 1s. a pair but
still as you say that's
only a call I never
sell a rabbit at 6d.
in course it costs more
my way in business is
to get 2d. profit &
the skin on every rabbit
it's the skins is the
profit now brings me from
1s. to 1s. 9d. a dozen
they're best in frosty weather
the fur's thickest then it
grows best in frost

XXVI

1

If I could do better
in the way of tin
in a country village
than in London why
I'd stick to the village

if the better tin lasted
for six months aye sir
for six years

what's places
to a man like me
between grub
& no grub

2

If I'm idle in the
country on a Sunday I
never go to church I
never was in a church
I don't know why my
silk handkerchief's worth more than
one of their smock-frocks
& quite as respectable

XXVII

1
Three yards a penny!
Three yards
a penny!

Beautiful songs! Newest songs!
Popular Songs!

Three yards a penny!

Song
song

songs!

2
I sometimes began
with singing or
trying to sing
I'm no vocalist the
first few words of any song
quite loud I'd begin

The Pope he leads a happy life
He knows no care

Buffalo gals come out to-night
Death of Nelson
The gay cavalier
Jim along Josey
There's a good time coming
Drink to me only
Kate Kearney
Chuckaroo-choo choo-choo-choot-lah
Chockala-roony-ninkaping-nang
Pagadaway-dusty-kanty-key
Hottypie-gunnypo-china-coo' that's a
Chinese song sir
I dreamed that I dwelt in marble halls
The standard bearer
Just like love
Whistle o'er the lave o't
Widow Mackree
I've been roaming
Oh! that kiss
The old English gentleman &c
&c &c

I dares say
they was all in the three yards

or was once

if they wasn't
there was others
as good

3
Some of the tunes there's
no act of parliament about
tunes you know sir was
stunners on the fiddle as
if a thousand bricks was
falling out of a cart

XXVIII

1

We are the
haristocracy of the streets

people don't pay us for what we gives 'em
but only to hear us talk we
live like yourself sir

by the hexercise of our hintellects

2

Why I'd go out now sir
with a dozen of Chigwell-rows
& earn my supper in half an hour
off of 'em

the murder of Sarah Holmes
at Lincoln is good too

that there
has been worked for the
last five year successively
every winter poor
Sarah Holmes bless her

She's saved me from
walking the streets all night
many a time

3
Some of the best of these
have been in work twenty years
the Scarborough murder has full
twenty years it's called
The Scarborough Tragedy
I've worked it myself it's
about a noble & rich young naval officer
seducing a poor clergyman's daughter
she is confined in a ditch
& destroys the child she is
taken up for it
tried & executed

this has had a great run it
sells all round the country places
& would sell now
if they had it out

mostly all our customers is females
they are the chief dependence we have the
Scarborough Tragedy is very attractive it
draws tears to the women's eyes to
think a poor clergyman's daughter

who is remarkably beautiful should
murder her own child it's
very touching to every feeling heart there's
a copy of verses with it too

4
Then there's the Liverpool Tragedy
that's very attractive it's
a mother murdering her own son
through gold he'd
come from the East Indies
& married a rich planter's daughter he
came back to England to
see his parents after an absence of
thirty years they kept a lodging-house
in Liverpool for sailors the son
went there to lodge &
meant to tell his parents
who he was in the morning his
mother saw the gold he had
got in his boxes & cut his throat
severed his head from his body
the old man upwards of seventy
holding the candle they
put a washing-tub under the bed
to catch his blood the morning after
the old man's daughter calls &
the old couple find they have

murdered their own son then
they both put an end to their
existence this is a
deeper tragedy than the
Scarborough Murder that suits
young people better they
like to hear about the young woman
seduced by the naval officer but
the mothers take more to
the Liverpool Tragedy it
suits them better

5
Pegsworth was an
out-and-out lot I
did tremendous with him
because it happened in London
down Ratcliff-highway that's a
splendid quarter for working there's
plenty of feelings but
bless you some places you go
you can't move no how

they've hearts like paving-stones
they wouldn't have the papers if you'd
give them
to 'em

especially when they
knows you

Greenacre didn't sell
so well as expected for
such a diabolical
out-and-out crime as
he committed but you see
he came close after Pegsworth &
that took the beauty off him

two murderers together is never
no good to nobody why
there was Wilson Gleeson
as great a villain as ever lived
went & murdered a whole family
at noon-day but
Rush coopered him
& likewise that girl at Bristol
made it no draw to any one

Daniel Good though
was a first-rater &
would have been much better
if it hadn't been for that there
Madam Toosow she
went down to Roehampton
& guv 2*l.* for the werry clogs as

he used to wash his master's carriage in so
in course
when the harristocracy
could go & see the real things the
werry identical clogs in the
Chamber of 'Orrors why
the people wouldn't look at
our authentic portraits of the
fiend in human form

6

the wife of the murdered man
kept the King's Head he was landlord on
open on the morning of the execution
& the place was like a fair I
even went & sold papers
outside the door myself I thought
if she war'n't ashamed
why should I be?

7

After that we had a fine fake
that was the fire of the Tower of London
it sold rattling we had about forty
apprehended for that
first we said two soldiers was
taken up that couldn't obtain their discharge
& then we declared it was a

well-known sporting nobleman
who did it for a spree

8
The boy Jones
in the Palace wasn't
much of an affair
for the running patterers

the ballad singers
or street screamers we calls 'em
had the pull out of
that

the patter
wouldn't take they'd
read it all in the
papers before

9
there was Rush I
lived on him for a month or more
I was 14s. in debt for rent

in less than fourteen days I
astonished the wise men in the east
paying my landlord
all I owed him

10

since Dan'el Good there'd
been little or nothing doing
in the murder line no one
could cap him
till Rush turned up a
regular trump for us I
went down to Norwich
expressly to work the execution
I worked my way down there
with *a sorrowful lamentation*
of his own composing I'd
got written by the blind man

on the morning of the execution
we beat all the regular
newspapers out of the field
for we had the full true
& particular account
down you see
by our own express
& that can beat anything
ever they can publish
we gets it printed several days
afore it comes off
& goes & stands with it
right under the drop
& many's the penny I've

turned away when
I've been asked for an
account of the whole business
before it happened so
you see for herly
& correct hinformation
we can beat the *Sun* aye
or the moon either

11
A slum's a paper fake
make a foot-note of
that sir I think Adelaide
was the first thing
I worked after I told you
of my tomfooleries

yes it was
her helegy she
weren't of no
account whatsomever
& Cambridge was
no better
nor Adelaide

but there was poor Sir
Robert Peel he
was some good as

good as 5s. a day to me
for four or five days
when he was freshest
browns were thrown
out of the windows
& one copper cartridge
was sent flying
with 13½d. in it
all copper as if
collected I worked
Sir Robert at the West End
in the quiet
streets & squares
certainly we had a
most beautiful helegy

well poor gentleman
what we earned on him
was some set-off to us
for his starting his new
regiment of the Blues
the Cook's Own

not that they've troubled me
much I was once
before Alderman Kelly
when he was Lord Mayor
charged with obstructing or

some humbug of that sort
what are you my man? says he
quietly & like a gentleman
in the same line as yourself
my lord says I
how's that? says he
I'm a paper-worker for my
living my lord says I

I was soon discharged

12
Sirrell was no good either
not salt to a herring though
we worked him in his own
neighbourhood & pattered
about gold & silver
all in a row Ah!
says one old woman
he was a 'spectable man
werry marm says I

13
Hollest weren't no good either
the murder came off badly

& you can't expect fellows
like them murderers to have

any regard for the interest of
art & literature

then there's so long to wait
between the murder & the trial
unless the fiend in human form
keeps writing beautiful love-letters
the excitement can't be kept up

the newspapers there's plenty of 'em
gets more & more
into our line they
treads in our footsteps sir they
follows our bright example

O! isn't there a nice rubbing
& polishing up

this here copy won't do
this must be left out &
that put in 'cause it
suits the walk of the paper

why you must know sir *I*
know don't tell me you
can't have been on the
Morning Chronicle for nothing

XXIX

No sir it wasn't only
working people that
bought of me but

merchants & their clerks
s'pose they took the papers
home with 'em

for their wives & families
which is a cheap
way of doing

as a newspaper costs
3*d*. at least but
stop sir stop there

wasn't no threepennies then
nothing under 6*d*.
if they wasn't more

can't just say but
it was better for us
when newspapers was

high I never
heard no sorrow expressed
not in the least

XXX

It was distress that first drove me to it

I had learnt to make willow bonnets but that branch of
trade went entirely out so

having a wife & children I was drove to write out a paper

The People's Address to the King on the Present State of
the Nation

I got it printed & took it into the streets & sold it

did very well with it & made 5s. a day while it lasted

I never was brought up to any mechanical trade my
father was a clergyman

it breaks my heart when I think of it

I have as good a wife as ever lived & I'd give the world to
get out of my present life it would be heaven to get away
from the place where I am

I'm obliged to cheer up my spirits

if I was to give way to it I shouldn't live long it's like
a little hell to be in the place where we live

associated with the ruffians that we are my distress
of mind is awful but

it won't do to show it at my lodgings they'd only
laugh to see me down-hearted so

I keep my trouble all to myself

oh I am heartily sick of this street work the insults
have to put up with the drunken men swearing

XXXI

1

Stop there sir stop
stop sir I
have had to say about
the Queen lately in coorse

nothing can be said
against her
& nothing ought to that's
true enough but

the last time she was
confined I cried her *accounchement*
of *three* Lord love you sir
it would have been no
use crying *one*
people's so used to
that but a Bobby came up
& he stops me & said
it was some impudence
about the Queen's
coachman
*w*hy look at it
says I fat-head I knew
I was safe & see if

there's anything in it about the
Queen or her coachman & he
looked & in coorse there was
nothing I forget
just now what
the paper *was* about

2
The speeches on the
opening of parliament
which the newspapers has ready
has no sale in the crowd
to what they had

I only sold two papers
at 6*d*. each
this last go

I ventured on no more or
should have been a loser

If the Queen isn't there
none's sold but we
always has a speech ready
as close as can be got
from what the morning papers
says one gent

says to me but

that ain't the real speech!

it's a far better says I

& so it is

3

If the *Times* was

cross-examined he

must confess he's

outdone though

he's a rich *Times*

& we is

poor fellows

XXXII

I've been in the streets ever since
& don't see how I could possibly get out of them

at first I felt a great degradation
at being driven to the life

I shunned grooms & coachmen
I might be known to

I didn't care for others
that sort of feeling wears out though

I'm a widower now & my family
feels as I did at first

what I'm doing is 'low'
they won't assist though

they may give me 1s now & then but
they won't assist me to leave the streets

they'll rather blame me for going into them
though there was only that

or robbing

or starving

XXXIII

Ah! once
I could
screeve a fakement or
cooper a monekur
with any man alive

& my heart's game now but

I'm old
& asthmatic
& got the rheumatics
so I ain't
worth a damn

XXXIV

Takes in all sorts & all sizes all
colours & all nations similar to
what's expected of the Crystal Palace

I was a *muck-snipe* when I was there

a man regularly done up
coopered & humped

& it was a busyish time
when the deputy paired off the single men
I didn't much like my bed-mate
a shabby-genteel buttoned up to the chin
& in the tract line I thought of
Old Seratch when I looked at him
though he weren't a Scotchman I think I
tipped the wink to an acquaintance there
told him I thought my old complaint
was coming on to kick & bite
like a horse in my sleep
a'cause my mother was terrified
by a wicious horse not
werry long afore I was born
so I dozed on the bed-side
& began to whinny & my bed-mate
jumped up frightened &
slept on the floor

XXXV

1
it's not all men
as has or
I shouldn't have been
waiting here on
you but
you has your
choice I
tell you

sleep there on that
shake-down or
turn out &
be damned

2
The windows
there sir are
not to let the
light in but
to keep the
cold out

3

Of course
they don't ask any couple
to show their marriage lines
no more than they do
any lord & lady
or one that ain't a lady
if she's with a lord
at any fash'nable hotel
at Brighton I've
done tidy well on
slums about ladies in a
Brighton hotel
just by the Steyne
werry tidy

4

Whatever that's
bad & wicked
that any one can
fancy could be
done in such places
among boys & girls
that's never been taught
or won't be taught better
is done
& night after night

5

A rackety place sir
one of the showfuls

a dicky one a
free-and-easy you can
get a pint of beer
& a punch of the head
all for 2*d*.

as for sleeping
on a Saturday night there O

no we
never mention it

6

Why in course sir
if you is in a country town
or village where there's only
one lodging-house &
that a bad one an
old hand can always
suit his-self in London you
must get half-drunk or your
money for your bed is
wasted there's so much rest

owing to you

after a hard day &

bugs & bad air'll

prevent its being paid

if you don't lay in some

stock of beer or liquor of some sort

to sleep on it's a duty

you owes yourself but

if you haven't the browns why

then in course you

can't pay it

7

When a man's lost caste he

may as well

go the whole hog

bristles & all

& a low lodging-house

is the entire pig

8

Brighton is a town where

there is a great many

furnished cribs

let to needys

that are

molled up

XXXVI

A few years back
an old woman kept a padding-ken the place
was well-known to the monkry

& you was reckoned flat if you hadn't been there

she was a strong Methodist

a queer method

there was thirty standing beds
besides make-shifts &
furnished rooms which were called cottages

the old woman when any female
old or young who had no tin
came into the kitchen
made up a match for her with some men
fellows half-drunk

there was always a broomstick at hand
& they was both made to jump over it

& that
was called a broomstick wedding

without that a couple weren't looked on as man and wife

in course
the man paid for the dos

XXXVII

We are fond of music nigger music was
very much liked among us but it's stale
now flash songs are liked & sailors' songs
patriotic songs costers listen very quietly to songs
they don't in the least understand we have
among us translations of the patriotic French songs
Mourir pour la patrie is very popular &
so is the Marseillaise a song to take
hold of us must have a good chorus
they like something that is worth hearing such
as the soldier's dream the dream of Napoleon
or I 'ad a dream an 'appy dream

XXXVIII

1

I've been a costermonger a lot-seller a nut-seller secret-
paper-seller

with straws you know sir

a cap-seller a street-printer cakeman clown

an umbrella-maker toasting-fork maker sovereign seller
& ginger-beer seller

I hardly know what I haven't been

I made my own when last I worked beer

Sunday was my best day Sunday mornings when
there's no public-houses open

drinking Saturday nights make dry Sunday mornings

many a time men have said to me let's have a bottle to
quench a spark in my throat my mouth's like an oven

I've had to help people lift the glass to their lips their
hands trembled so they couldn't have written their
names plain if there was a sovereign for it

but these was only chance customers

one or two in a morning & five or six on a Sunday
morning

2
I used to be off early on Sunday mornings
sometimes to Hackney Marsh & sell my beer there to
gentlemen
oldish gentlemen
some of them going a fishing others going there to swim

3
The harder you pumps the frothier it comes &
though it seems to fill a big glass
& the glass an't so big for holding as it looks
let it settle & there's only a quarter of a pint

4
men who looked as if they'd been on the loose all night

one gentleman looks sharp about him & puts a dark-
coloured stuff very likely it's brandy into the two or
three glasses of water which he drinks every Sunday

or which he used to drink rather for I missed him all last
summer I think

his hand trembled
like a aspen

5

Ah sir you should have seen
how a poor man last winter
swallowed a penn'orth

he'd been a-wandering all night he
said & he looked it & a gentleman
gave him 2*d* for he took pity on his

hungry look & he spent 1*d*. with me
& I gave him another cup for charity
God bless the gentleman & you!

says he it's saved my life
if I'd bought a penny loaf I'd have
choked on it he wasn't

a beggar for I never saw him before
& I've never seen him
from that day to this

6

No one will stop to drink elder wine
in the wet they'll rather have a pennor'th of gin or half

a pint of beer
with the chill off
under shelter

I start when I think the weather's cold enough a
sharp frosty dry day suits me best

& keep at it as long as there's any demand my
customers are boys & poor people & I sell
more ha'porths than pennor'ths

I've heard poor women that's bought of me say
it was the only wine they ever tasted

7
money goes I can't tell how
'specially if you drinks a drop as I do
sometimes
foggy weather
drives me to it
I'm so worritted

now & then you'll
mind sir

8

I've seen a baby of five year old reeling drunk in a
tap-room

his governor did it for the lark of the thing

to see him chuck hisself about

sillyfied like

XXXIX

1

Billingsgate's my best ground I
sell to the costers & roughs &
all the parties that has their dinners in tap-rooms

a bit of steak or
cold meat they've
brought with them

there's very little fish eat in Billingsgate except
perhaps at the ord'n'ries

I'm looked for as regular as dinner-time
landlords tell me to
give my customers plenty of
pepper & salt to
make them thirsty

I go on board the Billingsgate ships too
& sometimes sell 6d. worth
to captain & crew it's a treat
after a rough voyage

I go out
morning noon & night

& night I go my round
when people's having a bite of supper
in the public-houses I
sell to the women of the town

yes I give them credit

tonight now I expect to
receive 2*s*. 3*d*. or
near on it I've
trusted them this week they
mostly pay me on a Saturday night I
lose very little by them

2
I'm knocked about
in public-houses by the
Billingsgate roughs &
bilked by the prigs

3
There's often a good sale
when a public room's filled
people drinking there
always want to
eat they buy whelks
not to fill themselves but
for a relish a man

that's used to the trade
will often get off
inferior sorts to the lushingtons he'll
have them to rights

whelks is all the same
good bad or middling
when a man's drinking if they're
well seasoned with pepper & vinegar

Oh yes any whelk-man will
take in a drunken fellow
& do it all the same if he's
made up his mind to
get drunk hisself
that very night

3
Masters have sent out
their servant-maids to me for
three or four penn'orths for supper

I've offered the maids a whelk but
they won't eat them in the street

I dare say they're afraid

their young men may be about
& might think they wasn't ladies

XL

1

Yes sir I mind very well the first time as I ever sold ices

I don't think they'll ever take greatly in the streets but there's no saying

Lord! how I've seen the people splutter when they've tasted them for the first time

I did as much myself

they get among the teeth & make you feel as if you tooth-ached all over

one young Irish fellow from his look & cap a printer's or stationer's boy he bought an ice of me & when he'd scraped it all together with the spoon he made a pull at it as if he was a drinking beer

in course it was all among his teeth in less than no time & he stood like a stattey for a instant

& then he roared out Jasus! I'm kilt the could shivers is on to me!

but I said O you're all right you are

& he says what d'you mane you horrid horn
selling such stuff as that
an' you must have
the money first

bad scran to the likes o' you

2
We sees a many dodges in the streets sir
a many

I knew one smart servant maid
treated to an ice by her young man
& he soon was stamping with the ice among his teeth

but she knew how to take hern
put the spoon
right into the middle of her mouth &
when she'd had a clean swallow she says
O Joseph why didn't you ask
me to tell you
how to eat your ice

the conceit of sarvant gals is ridiculous

but it goes out of them when they gets married
& has to think of how to get broth before how to eat ices

3

One hot day about eleven
a thin tall gentleman
not very young
threw down 1*d*. to me
& says says he
as much ice as you can make
for that

he knew how to take it
when he'd done he says says he
by God my good feller
you've saved my life I've been
keeping it up all night
& I was dying of a burnt-up throat after a snooze
& had only 1*d*
so sick & hot was my stomach
I could have knelt down
& taken a pull at the Thames
we was near it at the time
you've saved my life &
I'll see you again but
I've never see'd him since

He was a gentleman I think

he was in black & wore a big black & gold ring

XLI

1

Mother's the
best name I'm called in a public-house
& it ain't a respectable name

here mother give us one of yer bloody trotters
is often said to me
the stuff'll choke me
but that's as good as the Union

he ain't a bad man though

he sometimes treats me he'll
bait my trotters but
that's his larking way
& then he'll say a pennorth o'gin'll
make your old body spin it's
his own poetry he says I
don't know
what he is but

he's often drunk

2

I've known a woman buy a trotter

put her teeth into it

then say it wasn't good

return it wasn't paid for

& because I grumbled

I was abused by her as if

I'd been a Turk

the landlord interfered & he said

said he I'll not have this poor woman

insulted she's here for the

convenience of them as

requires trotters

she's a well-conducted woman I'll

not have her insulted he says

says he lofty & like a gentleman sir

why who's insulting the old bitch

says the woman says she

she wasn't a woman of the town

as used me so

plenty of

them knows what poverty is

& is civiler poor things yes
I'm sure of that though
it's a shocking life O shocking

3
I never go to the
playhouse-door but on a fine
night young men treats their
sweethearts to a trotter for
a relish with a drop
of beer between the acts

XLII

Love & murder suits us best sir

but these few years I think there's a great deal more
liking for deep tragedies among us

they set men a thinking but then

we all consider them too long

Hamlet we can make neither end nor side of & nine out
of ten of us aye far more than that would like it to be
confined to the ghost scenes the funeral & the killing
off at the last

Macbeth would be better liked if it was only the witches
& the fighting

we always stay to the last because we've paid for it
all or very few costers would see a tragedy out if any
money was returned after two or three acts

we can't tumble to that barrikin

XLIII

I've known women that seemed working men's
or little shopkeeper's wives
buy of me & ask
which of my stuffs took greatest hold of the breath

I always knew what they was up to
they'd been having a drop & didn't want it detected why

it was only last Saturday week
two niceish-looking niceish-dressed women
comes up to me
& one was going to buy peppermint-rock
& the other says to her don't
you fool he'll only think you've been
drinking gin-&-peppermint
coffee takes it off best so
I lost my customers

they hadn't had a *single* drain that night I'll go bail

but still

they didn't look like regular lushingtons at all

XLIV

Boys & girls is
my best customers for cruds sir

perhaps I sell to them almost
half of all I get rid of

very little fellows will treat girls
often bigger than themselves & they
have as much chaffing & nonsense
about it's being stunning good for the teeth
& such like as if they was grown-up

some don't much like it at first but they
gets to like it

one boy whose young woman made faces at it
& it *was* a little sour to be sure that morning
got quite vexed & said
wot a image you're a-making on yourself!

they're the street-boys mostly

XLV

That

       brandishing something in his face

that's what licks them

it don't matter whether I was one of Lot's daughters
afore I might have been
awful I don't say I wasn't
but I'm his wife &
this 'ere's
what licks 'em

XLVI

1

I always dress well

at least you
mayn't think so but
I am always neat &
respectable & clean

if the things I have on
ain't worth the sight of money
some women's things cost them

2

Ah sir
a neat gown
does a deal with a man he
always likes a girl best
when everybody else
likes her too

3

The women doesn't show their necks
as I've seen the ladies do
in them there pictures of
high life in the shop-winders or
on the stage

their Sunday gowns
which is their dancing gowns
ain't made
that way

4
the gals
axully liked a feller for
walloping them

as long as the bruises hurted
she was always
thinking on the cove as
gived 'em her

5
Now there's a gal I knows
as came to me
no later than this here week &
she had a dreadful swole face & a
awful black eye

& I says who's done that
& she says says she why
Jack

just in that way

& then she says
says she I'm going to
take a warrant out
to-morrow

well he gets the warrant
that same night but she
never appears again him
for fear of
getting more beating

6
The first step to ruin is them
places of penny gaffs
for they hears things
there as oughtn't to be
said to young gals

Besides the lads is
very insinivating
& after leaving them places
will give a gal a drop of
beer & make her half tipsy
& then they
makes their arrangements

I've often heerd the boys boasting of
having ruined gals

for all the world as if they

was the first noblemen in the land

7

our togs is

in the latest

fashion of

Petticoat-lane

brass buttons like

a huntman's with

foxes' heads on em

looked stunning flash

& the gals liked em

8

If I seed my gal

a talking to another chap I'd

fetch her sich a

punch of the nose as should

plaguy quick

stop the whole business

XVII

1

my father was
I've heard say a
well-known swell of capers gay who
cut his last fling with great applause or

if you must know I heard
he was hung
for killing a man committing a burglary

in other words he was
a macing-cove what robs

& I'm his daughter worse luck

2

Birth is the result of accident the merest
chance in the world whether you're
born a countess or a washerwoman

I'm neither

only a mot who does a little
typographing by way of variety

those who have had good nursing & all that

& the advantages of a sound education

who have a position to lose

prospects to blight

relations to dishonour

may be blamed for going on the loose but

I'll be hanged if priest or moralist

is to come down on

me with the

sledge-hammer of their denunciation

XLVIII

1

He first brought me to
Simpson's hotel in the Strand where
we had dinner then
took me to the opera

we went to Scott's supper rooms in the Haymarket
we walked up & down the Haymarket

he took me to several of the cafes
we had wine & refreshments

about four o'clock in the morning he
called a Hansom & drove me
to his house & there

2

I ain't very good with my needle at fine needlework
& the slopsellers won't have me

I would have slaved for them though
bad as they do pay you
& hard as you must work

to get enough to live on
& poor living God knows at that

I feel very miserable for what I've done but

I was driven to it indeed I was sir

I daren't tell father he'd curse me at first

though he might forgive me

afterwards though he's poor he's

always been honest

& borne a good name but now

3

After I had parted with my jewellery

& most of my clothes I

walked in the Haymarket

& went to the Turkish divans

Sally's & other cafes &

restaurants

Soon after

I became unfortunate

& had to part with the

remainder of my

dresses

since then I've been

more shabby in appearance &

not so much noticed

XLIX

The women of the town are good customers

at least they are in the Cut

& Shoreditch

if they have five-penn'orth
when they're treated perhaps
there's always sixpence

they'll want credit sometime I've
given trust to a woman of that sort
far as 2*s.* 6*d.* I've
lost very little by them

those women's good pay
take it altogether they
know how hard it is to get a crust &
have a feeling for a poor man
if they haven't for a rich one

L

I comes out in the Parks sir
at night sometimes
when I've 'ad a bad day
& ain't made above a few pence

which ain't enough to
keep us as we should be kept
I mean sir the children
should have a bit of meat
& my ole man & me
wants some blue ruin to
keep our spirits up so

I'se druv to it sir
by poverty &

nothink on the face of God's blessed earth sir
shouldn't have druv me but that

for the poor babes must live
& who 'as they to look to but
their ard-working misfortunate mother

which she is now talking to your honour

& won't yer give a poor woman a 'apny sir
I've seven small children at home
& my 'usban's laid with the fever you
won't miss it yer honour
only a 'apny for a poor woman as
ain't ad a bit of bread between her teeth since
yesty morning I ax yer parding

LI

Now those poor things
that walks down there

they're often customers but
not near so good
as they was ten year ago no indeed

nor six or eight year

they like something that
bites in the mouth such as
peppermint-rock or
ginger-drops

they used to buy a penn'orth or two
& offer it to people
but they don't now I think

I've trusted them ha'pennies
& pennies sometimes
they always paid me

some that held their heads high like
might say I really have no change I'll
pay you to-morrow

she hadn't no change poor lass

sure enough & she hadn't

nothing to change either I'll go bail

The London Scavenger

[*From a Daguerreotype by* Beard]

LII

Times is altered sir
since I come on the town I can
remember when all the
swells used to come down hereaway
instead of going to the Market

those times is past they is

worse luck like myself
nothing lasts for ever I've
stood my share of wear & tear

wish they might come again but

wishing's no use

> She would not go to the workhouse and she could
> get no work to do

> she could sew and she could paint in water-colours
> but she was afraid to be alone she could not sit
> hours and hours by herself her thoughts distracted
> her and drove her mad

> She once thought of turning Roman Catholic and
> getting admitted into a convent

she did not think she would live long she
had injured her constitution so greatly she
had some internal disease she didn't know
what it was but a hospital surgeon told her
it would kill her in time

and she had her moments generally hours of
oblivion when she was intoxicated which she
always was when she could get a chance

if she got ten shillings from a drunken man
either by persuasion or threats she would not
come to the Park for days until all her money
was spent

on an average she came three times a week or
perhaps twice always on Sunday a good day

You folks as has honour
& character & feelings & such
can't understand how all
that's been beaten out of
people like me

I don't feel I
aren't happy either

it isn't happiness

I get enough money to
keep me in victuals
& drink

& it's the drink mostly
keeps me going you've no idea
how I look forward to my drop of gin it's
everything to me

I don't suppose I'll live much longer
that's another thing that
pleases me I don't
want to live & yet

I don't care enough about dying to
make away with myself

I aren't got
that amount of feeling
some has

LIII

I once went to school
for a couple of weeks
but the cove used to
fetch me a wipe over
the knuckles with his stick
I wasn't going to stand
that there why you see
I aint no great schollard

LIV

1

Byron Lord Byron's
latest and best po'ms
Sixpence! Sixpence!

Eightpence!

I take penny bids
under a shilling

Eightpence for the poems
written by a lord

Gone!

Yours sir

2

Coop'r Coop'r!
published at 3s. 6d.

as printed on the back

superior to Byron
Coop'r's Task

No bidders?

Thank you sir
One-and-six

your's sir

3
Young

Young's Night Thoughts
Life Death and Immortality
great subjects
London edition

marked 3*s*. 6*d*.

Going!

last bidder

two shillings

gone

4

The Rambler!

Now you rambling boys now

You young devils
that's been staring those pretty
girls out of countenance
here's the very book for you
& more shame for you
& me too but I must sell I must
do business if any lady or
gen'lman'll stand treat
to a glass of brandy and water
warm with
I'll tell more about this Rambler
I'm too bashful as it is

Who bids?
Fifteen-pence
thank'ee sir

Sold again!

The Rambler

was Dr. Johnson's!

5

Here is the History of the
Real Flying Dutchman
& *no* mistake

no fiction I
assure you
upon my honour

published at 10*s.*
who bids half-a-crown?

Sixpence

thank you sir

Ninepence going
going!

Any more?

gone!

LV

1

only last Monday and Wednesday
both very rainy days
I took only 5*d*. I
didn't take more than 5*d*.

& I leave you to
judge the living I shall
clear out of that

& I know the man with the catalogue
at another place
didn't take 1*d*.

it's sad work sir
as you stand in the wet and cold
with no dinner for yourself
& no great hope of taking one
home to your family

2

Why there was a volume
lettered Pamphlets &
I think there *was* something about Jack Sheppard in it

but it was all odds and ends of other things

here's the *real* Jack Sheppard
sings out the man
& no gammon the real edition
no spooniness here but set off with
other interesting histories
valuable for the rising generation
& all generations this is the
real Jack this will
put you up to the time o' day
nix my dolly pals bid away

well sir the man didn't do well
perhaps he cleared 1*s*. 6*d*.
or a little more that evening on books

people laughed more than they bought

but it's no wonder the trade's going to the dogs
they're not allowed to have a pitch now

I shouldn't be surprised if they wasn't
all driven out of London next year it's
contrary to Act of Parliament
to get an honest living
in the streets
now-a-days

LVI

1

when I was a lad at school
there was Jews used to go about
with boxes on their backs
offering rings & pencil-cases
& lots of things
that's no real use to nobody
& they told everybody they
sold everything & us boys
used to say then
give's a ha'porth of boiled treacle

it was a regular joke

wish I'd
stuck more to my book then
but

what can't be cured
must be endured you know

2

There's not a few people who
stand & read & read
for half an hour or

an hour at a time it's
very trying to the temper
when they take up room that way

prevent others seeing the works

never lay out a penny theirselves but

they seem quite lost in a book

some seem very poor
judging by their dress &
some seem shabby genteels

customers of this sort
who aren't customers
I can't help telling them
when I see them going
I'm much obliged
& I hope that
perhaps next time they'll
manage to say thank ye for
they don't open their lips
once in twenty times

3

Why yes sir

I *can* read

& write but

it's been no

good to me

LVII

Yes indeed you
all come to
such as me at last

why last night I
heard a song
about all the
stateliest buildings
coming to the ivy

& I thought
as I listened it was
the same with authors

the best that the
best can do is the
book-stall's food
at last and no harm
for he's in the best of
company with
Shakespeare &
all the great people

LVIII

Why sir I myself have
slept in the top room
of a house not far from
Drury-lane

you could study the stars
if you were so minded
through the holes
a fine summer's night
& the openings in the roof
were an advantage they
admitted air I
never went there again

you may judge what thoughts
went through a man's mind

a man who had
seen prosperous days

as he lay in a place like that

without being able to sleep

watching the sky

LIX

I haven't seen anything of him sir
for a long while

I dare say he was some
poor musicianer or
singer

or a reduced gentleman
perhaps

for he
always came after dusk

or else on bad dark days

The Sewer-Hunter

[From a Daguerreotype by Beard *]*

Publisher's Note

We have appended a substantial section of an exchange in the spring of 2006 between Edmund Hardy and John Seed about Pictures from Mayhew. *It was initially published in the* Intercapillary Space *blogzine. We are grateful to Edmund Hardy and the* Intercapillary Space *team for permission to print it here.*

E.H.: In your close listening to the voices in *Mayhew*, did you sense an ethical responsibility to these people? Could you say something about your conception of form here. Is it an ethics of structuring and restructuring textual evidence?

J.S.: Yes I did feel a kind of ethical responsibility and it did, as you suggest, have implications for the form of the work.

I was uncomfortable. I didn't want to put words into other peoples' mouths. Mayhew was sometimes accompanied by a shorthand writer who took down interviews. Sometimes he made his own notes of interviews. These were then transformed by him into coherent prose. After all, people don't actually talk in prose – in a single long line broken up into coherent sentences! They talk in highly fragmented, disconnected, hesitant lines of verse! So I suppose my work of reading/writing was partly about undoing Mayhew's own work of rewriting and perhaps getting closer to his listening and recording.

I didn't add anything. I simply cut punctuation, cut what sounded like padding and undid some degree of grammatical order. I arranged the material into lines. Sometimes I did this in a form which caught the rhythms and pauses of the speaking voice. But I didn't want this to become a habit and many sections work against the sound of the speaking voice. I wanted the form to slow down the reader -- to draw attention to the actual words and the patterns they made. So I played around with the arrangement – three words to a line, or five words to a line or whatever. Or divided up the writing up into verses. I wanted to play with other kind of relations between words, including their visible form on the white paper. I tried not to slip into a single method, section by section. I tried to keep moving, to keep changing, to keep defamiliarising – for myself as much as for any reader.

I avoided titles and subtitles, creating numbered sections which are not easy to navigate around. This was intended to amplify the cacophony of strange voices and thus maximise the work the reader has to do to make sense. A few readers have complained how difficult they have found it to make their way around those 160 or more pages – how hard it is to go back to a remembered section. They complained they felt a bit lost. They wanted titles and subtitles. They also wanted footnotes and explanations for some of the words and references. I was delighted to be so unhelpful.

I was also aware of an ethics of responsibility in terms of avoiding aestheticising brutal realities and painful experiences. Mayhew certainly doesn't do that – though I'm not sure he entirely escapes the charge of sensationalising his material, especially in some of the later work where he turns his attention to prostitutes. There are also moments of sentimentalising and even, on occasion, moralising. No doubt I've not always been responsive to these limitations – and I may have added others of my own.

E.H.: We are always aware that Reznikoff's *Testimony* takes place before the law – legal dialects and the high proportion of conflicts or accidents – whereas here I get a different sense of "being before" from the two Prefaces, that Mayhew – and we the reader – are spies or, worse, administrators. Could you comment on the possibilities let loose in the book of a group of people held as subjects "before sociology"?

J.S.: I hope these people are not 'held' anywhere as subjects, or objects, of somebody else's knowledge. My two short prefaces are there to place the "author" and the reader in an uncomfortable position. "We" are looking at "them". But they are looking right back at us and maybe they don't much like what they see. In a sense Mayhew is indeed a spy for the state. Elsewhere in the text too there are occasional moments of that kind of confrontation between author and reader on the one hand and these people who have a voice and a consciousness on the other. I hope they are subjects in the sense of being an active 'I' in their own sentences, often (but not always) resistant to incorporation into any higher order of meanings, questioning from within the very text which represents them – or mis-represents them. So the text doesn't try to smooth out these tensions.

I hope *Pictures from Mayhew* undermines any reader-position as being the bearer of knowledge (whether sociology or anything else) of other people as objects. One of the fascinating things about reading Mayhew is to watch his doubts and uncertainties gathering as the people he talks to challenge his every assumption. He had the capacity to question his most basic presuppositions and try, painfully, to develop new ones. He learned that he really didn't know better. Few other contemporary commentators on working-class life in Victorian London had that kind of negative capability, that courage to persist in uncertainty.

I should say how much I admire Reznikoff's writing. I corresponded with him in the early 70s and still have several lovely letters he wrote to me. But I wonder if *Testimony* doesn't subscribe to the notion that accurate use of language and close reading of evidence can somehow capture what actually happened, the truth or the reality outside language. I teach and write history but I don't think I can share that position very easily. Anyway, in *Pictures from Mayhew* representation of some kind of event or object is not, usually, what I'm doing. I'm interested in working with this recorded speech to see what happens inside it, rather than moving out from it to 'the real'. I think a number of different things do happen – which probably make this text more engaging for those interested in poetry than for those interested in nineteenth-century history.

E.H.: Why do you think oral history seems closely related to a left-wing politics?

J.S.: I'm not sure oral history is always closely related to a left-wing politics, not necessarily so anyway. I suppose in Britain some of its origins were in the 1930s, in the work of the Mass Observation people, which has always fascinated me. And some of them were interested in poetry, (Charles Madge), and in other innovative forms of writing (Humphrey Jennings's *Pandaemonium*). Another impulse comes from the ideas of 'history from below' in the 1960s and the work of E.P.Thompson, Raphael Samuel and the History Workshop Movement. Raphael Samuel's *East End Underworld: Chapters in the Life of Arthur Harding*, published in 1981, is an amazing experiment in oral history. At the core of this kind of history writing was the idea that working people themselves should be writing their own history – not university-educated professional historians. Oral history was just one method of trying to elicit some kind of democratic or people's history. Raphael Samuel spent most of his working life at Ruskin College in Oxford. And E.P.Thompson worked in Adult Education for many years while he was writing *The Making of the English Working Class* (1963). Mayhew was an important source and example for E.P.Thompson of course: he co-edited an important Penguin collection, *The Unknown Mayhew*, in 1973. His introduction is very helpful.

But there is a great deal of oral history which would refuse any kind of left-wing political affiliation. And even some of the above could be represented as a kind of spying by the authorities. Michel de Certeau, for instance, argued this kind of case against 'left-wing' explorations of the popular in an essay in his *Heterologies*. Maybe the investigating policeman is a kind of oral historian too? And maybe those who were suspicious of Mayhew and his questions had a point!

E.H.: *Pictures From Mayhew* seems metaphysical in that it brings out from Mayhew an almost timeless milieu – or a re-selection designed for now? – I kept thinking about contemporary mega-cities and the continuing migrations of people who become the urban poor there, pursuing similar livelihoods to the ones described, whereas reading the Mayhew, the extra details keep one's thoughts on London more firmly.

J.S.: I have an almost visceral recoil away from any notion of the timeless, though I note you do say *'almost* timeless'. Phew! What you point to are certain historical continuities in the character of national and now international labour markets. Labourers migrate and they often have to scratch a living in inhospitable city streets. Most of Mayhew's people had migrated into London from the rural counties of south-east England, though there were some, notably the Irish, who had come from further afield. Across the planet now migrants travel much further. And I'm sure that today conditions and kinds of work and social relations in many cities across the world – including the cities of the United States – resemble Mayhew's London in certain respects. Maybe London today is a lot more like Mayhew's London than it was between the 1920s and the 1970s? You'll have noted the final lines of the whole book?

cold night I feel
the cold of that night
in my limbs still
I thought it never
would be over

There is no full stop there either. And it *isn't* over. And if it is *never* over that isn't because it is "the human condition" or some other metaphysical alibi for the way things are.

Printed in the United Kingdom
by Lightning Source UK Ltd.
122703UK00001BA/5/A